# the roses and their thorns

Jasmitha Alle

# Contents

**Introduction**
    AUTHOR'S NOTE    1
    FOREWORD    3
**Love**    **7**
    Your thoughts    12
    Forever    15
    Nothing like you    17
    My one    20
    Lost    23
    Let go    27
    Yet again    30
    You are no more    32
    Pain    35
    Cold    36
**Friendship**    **50**
    With you, I'm home    54
    Beyond your mask    60
    Yesterday    63
    Today    66
**Society**    **80**
    Meh    82
    Used to it    85
    Silence    91

| | |
|---|---:|
| **Warmth** | 102 |
|     Spring | 103 |
|     Summer | 104 |
|     Monsoon | 105 |
|     Winter | 106 |
|     Life | 113 |
|     Paths unseen | 115 |
|     Time | 119 |
|     Regret | 124 |
|     Rewind | 128 |
|     The end | 132 |
| **Conclusion** | **138** |
| **Acknowledgement** | **139** |
| **ABOUT THE AUTHOR** | **143** |
| **CONNECT WITH THE POET** | **144** |

*the roses and their thorns*

# AUTHOR'S NOTE

In the quiet moments between the lines, within the echoes of every stanza, this collection finds its heartbeat. I embarked on this poetic journey with a heart full of empathy for the struggles that color our daily lives. The inspiration behind these verses is drawn from the problems that people encounter each day.
Life has its own music, and within its melodies, we often find ourselves struggling to maintain our authenticity in a world that can be quick to judge. It's in these moments of vulnerability that our strength is truly tested. This book, in its own humble way, seeks to remind us that despite the challenges and the voices that might deter us, our path is our own. Every step forward, no matter how small, is a triumph of resilience.

As you delve into these pages, I invite you to walk alongside the emotions that pulse through them. Whether you find solace in the familiarity of shared struggles or find strength in the verses that encourage you to persevere, my hope is that these poems become companions for your journey.

May these words resonate with you, reminding you that you are not alone in your battles. Every challenge you face is a testament to your strength, and every moment of doubt can be met with the unwavering certainty that you are on the path meant for you.

*Jasmitha Alle*

Thank you for embarking on this poetic odyssey with me. It's my sincere wish that these verses find a place in your heart and serve as a reminder that even amid the chaos, your story matters, and your resilience is a beacon of hope.

With gratitude,
Jasmitha Alle

# FOREWORD

In a world where cultural norms rule human existence, *the roses and their thorns* invites readers on an evocative journey through the intricacies of love, friendship, heartbreak, life's challenges, and the weight of societal expectations. With a diverse symphony of tones, ranging from the melancholic to the uplifting, this collection of verses resonates with a mix of emotions that touch the core of the human experience.

Through each verse, this book speaks directly to those who have traversed the landscapes of heartbreak, lost cherished friendships, and felt the crushing weight of societal norms. These poems extend a compassionate hand to anyone seeking solace, understanding, and connection within the labyrinth of their own feelings.

Amidst the shadows of melancholy, readers will find a mirror to their own struggles, reflecting the hardships that shape our paths. Yet, this collection is not a lamentation but a celebration of resilience. It reaches beyond sorrow to offer verses of hope, lifting the spirit and encouraging the soul to find the strength to rebuild.

The book embraces the complexities of existence, recognizing that life's beauty often lies in its challenges.

*Jasmitha Alle*

As readers navigate through the ebb and flow of emotions, they will be reminded that despite the trials and tribulations it is our response to adversity that defines us.

*the roses and their thorns*

The roses and their thorns gently impart the message that life, though rife with hardship, is also an opportunity to craft our own narratives and emerge stronger with an enduring spirit.

*Jasmitha Alle*

*the roses and their thorns*

# Love

*Jasmitha Alle*

We are all connected.
We are humans, after all.

*the roses and their thorns*

We are separated by a thin wall, and sometimes,
we only need some light to bring us together.

*Jasmitha Alle*

It's during those times when you can't sleep,
because reality is finally more beautiful than dreams.

*the roses and their thorns*

Million feelings but zero words.

*Jasmitha Alle*

## Your thoughts

My mind wanders and stumbles upon your thoughts again.
Day and night, they can't be fought,
Your smile, your eyes, they're etched in my heart,
Nothing can make me feel the way you do tonight.

My mind wanders and stumbles upon your thoughts again.
I can't help but wonder what I'd find,
If I could just reach out to your hand and hold them close to mine,
Nothing would ever matter to me more than this.

My mind wanders and stumbles upon your thoughts again.
What is it about you that's holding on to me so tight?
Is it your smile, so gentle and pleasant?
Or is it your eyes, so deep and true?

My mind wanders and stumbles upon your thoughts again.
Sometimes I wonder if you think of me too,
If you have any idea what I go through.
I'm imprisoned in this constant feeling I've never known

*the roses and their thorns*

My mind wanders and stumbles upon your thoughts again.
I can't escape this longing in my heart.
Maybe someday, I'll find the courage to say,
How much I care about you, in my own special way.

*Jasmitha Alle*

And that light finally united us.

## Forever

Cotton candy skies, petals fluttering in the wind.
Standing in front of me with a bouquet of black roses,
Your eyes holding a million words, a million secrets,
It felt as if time stood still just to watch us bloom.

Painting my life with your smile and grace,
Every moment with you, a cherished embrace.
Lost in your gaze, a million feelings take flight,
Whispering songs of love, as the stars envy us.

The world slowly fading with every heartbeat,
Leaving just the two of us in a moment so sweet.
The fireflies flickering around in delight,
Witnessing a love that only we know.

*Jasmitha Alle*

The light gently whispered the story our souls were meant to live.

*the roses and their thorns*

# Nothing like you

Sunflowers swaying in the wind,
The sun so bright, the bees buzzing,
Adding to the mellow mood,
Yet nothing as radiant as you.

A beautiful purple dusk,
Birds flying back to their nests, the crickets chirping,
Adding to the tranquility,
Yet nothing as serene as you.

A pitch-black sky,
The moon peeking through the clouds,
The stars dazzling impressively,
Yet nothing as stunning as you.

A pleasing pink dawn,
The sun still blushing behind the hills,
The dew still in the mood for some hide and seek,
Yet nothing as charming as you.

*Jasmitha Alle*

A house far away from the city,
Waking up to the birds singing,
Breathing the scent of the verdant beings,
Yet nothing as comforting as your smile.

A colorful fall,
The leaves lighting up the streets,
The season of love spreading its wings,
Yet nothing as warm as you.

A blue, cloudy morning,
Snow piling up by the front door,
Creating memories that I can cherish forever,
Yet nothing as memorable as you.

*the roses and their thorns*

In your eyes,
I discovered the map to a world,
where forever told things,
only our hearts could understand.

In your presence,
time loses its grip,
and the only reality is the infinity of you and me.

In your embrace,
I found the universe I never knew existed.

*Jasmitha Alle*

## My one

The sky changing every minute,
From bright orange to pastel pink,
Birds going back to their nests,
And the sun setting in the ocean.

Endless blue skies, clear reflections,
Nothing stopping us from soaring.
Your eyes, clear of thick clouds,
The reason behind my smile.

In the midst of all this,
My mind is engulfed, like a cloudy sky.
Clear and pure in essence,
But overcast by distress.

I look up to your black orbs,
Reflecting a million colors.
They hold my portrait,
Painted in each of its shades.

Just by looking into those eyes,
I feel better.
Just by looking into those eyes,
I know you're my one.

*the roses and their thorns*

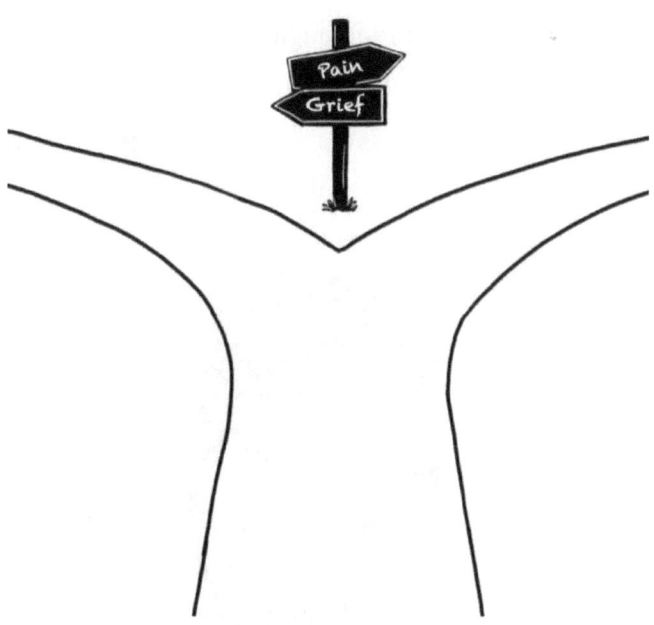

But our forever came to an end,
our love died,
our paths led us to different destinies.

*Jasmitha Alle*

From laughter that painted the skies,
to tears that now blur the stars we once knew,
our journey took a turn.

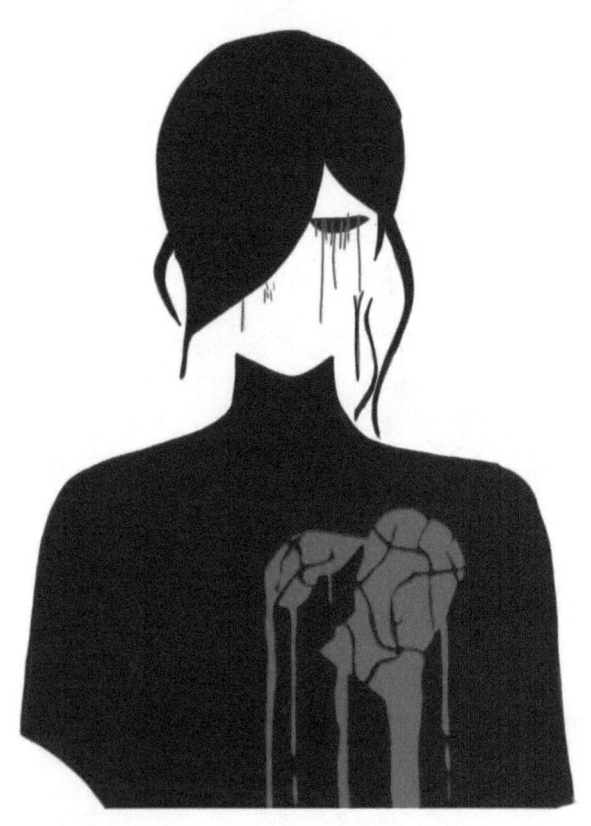

## Lost

Filled all these pages with your portraits,
Only for you to tear it apart without glancing even once.
Filled my heart with your little laughs,
Only for you to break it like it meant nothing.

Everywhere I look, all I see is you.
What do I do if this path looks shattered without you?
You're the light that always guided me,
Now my path is lost in the shadows of our smiles.

Never dreamt about a life without you,
But now you're a meaningless memory.
Looked for you in the darkest of places,
But I'm hopeless now, will you ever come back?

*Jasmitha Alle*

It's all fine until I see your shadows in my room again,
until I hear you calling my name from the backyard,
until I realize you're not really there,
and it's just my heart playing tricks on me.

*the roses and their thorns*

I'm a dream that has conquered sleep
to make you smile.
But, will I ever belong to your eyes?
Will I ever reside in your sight?

*Jasmitha Alle*

Time carved smiles on us,
but it's now etching the ache of
*What used to be.*

*the roses and their thorns*

## Let go

In the depths where exquisite memories reside,
A pile of bitter sorrows also lives unapproved.

A rainy night, fogged up windows, staring into the void,
Thoughts flowing in endlessly, wishing it never happened.
Wishing these thoughts would just disappear one day,
Like a meandering path that vanishes in the mist.

I have to accept it. I have to let go,
For some trees I thought were perennial,
Only held their beauty for a season,
Showing their true colors as time passed.

This moment, I don't want to let go,
But deep inside me echoes a voice,
A voice urging me to abandon this feeling,
Though my heart insists on staying.

Countless memories, never-ending laughter,
But it seems like forever is now coming to an end.
A lot of good chapters, but it's time to let go of this,
And move on to the next chapter waiting for me.

*Jasmitha Alle*

"Let go."

What do I do if fate always gives me things to let go?

I hate how I still look for you in the hallways,
I hate how I still strain to pick out your voice among others,
I hate that I still long for your presence, day after day.
I hate how I say I hate you,
though I know it's not true.

*the roses and their thorns*

Maybe we didn't have what it takes.
Maybe I was trying too hard to be the one for you,
that I lost myself,
the one you felt safe around,
the one you truly loved.

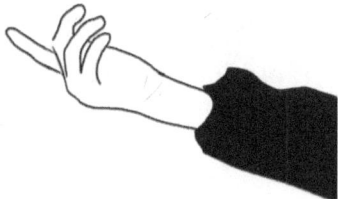

## Yet again

Just like how the thick, dark gray clouds indicated a storm,
So did my inner soul, another heartbreak,
But little did I know that, yet again,
I fell in love with someone I can't have.

Just like the leaves that drop during fall,
So did the joy in me, with no hope of regrowing my leaves,
Little did I know that, yet again,
I fell in love with someone I can't have.

Just like how dandelions are beautiful only until the wind blows,
One minute, I'm happy, and the next, I'm crying.
Little did I know that, yet again,
I fell in love with someone I can't have.

Just like how the earthy smell of mud leads to rain,
This will lead me to another sad song.

*the roses and their thorns*

Little did I know that, yet again,
I fell in love with someone I can't have.

Many sad stories, but this one feels like the saddest,
Many shades of blue, but this one is the darkest.
Little did I know that, yet again,
I fell in love with someone I can't have.

Tears.
The more I try to hold them in,
the more they try to escape.
Little did I know you're just like them.

*Jasmitha Alle*

## You are no more

I found you a while ago.
Remember us walking down the streets?
I think you wanted to be free,
And now, you are no more.

I screamed, cried, but what's the use,
When you've already decided to never return?
I think you wanted me to let you loose,
And for the same, you are no more.

I've been a chameleon for you since that day,
Changing every day just to feel loved again.
But you have already found your excuse,
And now, you are no more.

You told me you'll always be there.
Was that just a tale you told?
Do you think leaving me is fair?
And now, you are no more.

*the roses and their thorns*

Don't you think I deserve a chance?
I'll always be waiting for you,
But when will you realize it?
And still, you are no more.

I know you'll never come back,
But is it wrong of me to love you?
This world without you has turned black,
And forever, you are no more.

You can only speak, but I can hear too,
I have already become this weak,
What else do you seek?
And, you are no more.

Please grant my last wish.
Can you wave at me, smiling, as a last goodbye,
Before I leave you forever?
And after that, I am no more.

*Jasmitha Alle*

I am trying,

to let you go forever,

to find peace in this change,

but all my heart can remember,

is the moments we shared, the love we had,

your smile, your laugh, the way you truly cared.

## Pain

Overcast skies, withered flowers forlorn,
Our destiny now lost in the abyss, hopeless.
Those million secrets bound to haunt me,
It feels as if time stood still to watch us grieve.

Painting my life with blues and tears,
Every moment with you, a nail in my heart.
A million feelings, yet nothing could staunch the ache,
Yelling inaudible cries of apology as the stars pity me.

My heartbeat slowly fading away,
Leaving me alone in a moment so painful.
The fireflies fallen, like emotions extinguished,
Witnessing a sad story that only I know.

## Cold

Your silence growing louder every minute,
Your warmth escaping through the gaps you've created,
Your scent, different than mine now, that of a wilted flower,
Your light, slowly becoming darker than ever, closing in on me.

Your smile, as innocent as a beautiful bud,
Unfurling to be an evanescent blossom.
Your eyes, overcast with clouds, unsure,
Your love, gradually fading into the abyss.

The grief behind my smile will never disappear,
Like a curse, clinging on to me, unbridled.
Maybe these days were meant to fade away,
Maybe this is what forever always meant.

But even so, you're my one.

*the roses and their thorns*

Maybe one day you'll come back to me,
just as the birds return to their nests,
once dawn breaks.

*Jasmitha Alle*

> Or,
> am I dreaming again?

*the roses and their thorns*

"I will never leave you,"
the words etched onto my heart,
the same heart that is now scattered,
like the pieces of an incomplete puzzle,
with no hope of feeling complete ever again.

"I love you forever and always,"
maybe these words will find their meaning one day,
when forever dissolves in these tears of sorrow,
when forever is lost in the echoes of those muffled screams,
when forever crumbles like the ashes of a fading memory.

*the roses and their thorns*

It's hard to turn the page,
when you know someone
won't be there
in the next chapter.

Were you only worth a chapter in my story?

*the roses and their thorns*

Were all those promises meant to last only until the end of this chapter?

*Jasmitha Alle*

Wouldn't that mean that all my struggles to make us last forever were worth nothing?

*the roses and their thorns*

I just don't want to cry everytime you hurt me,
I just want to get you off my head.
I just want the wounds to heal soon.

*Jasmitha Alle*

We're
    just
        meant
            to
                be
                    you
                        and
                            me.
We were never meant to be one.

*the roses and their thorns*

Find someone who will light up the darkest part of you, darling;
not someone who will build a tombstone for a part of your soul.

*Jasmitha Alle*

*the roses and their thorns*

*Jasmitha Alle*

# Friendship

*the roses and their thorns*

It doesn't take a lifetime for things to change,
.
.
.
.
.
.
.
.
.
.
.
.
.
.
.
.
.
.
.
.
.
.
.
.
.
.
.
All it takes is a moment.

*Jasmitha Alle*

And amidst the chaos of life's endless maze,

you whispered softly,

in an unexpected way.

*the roses and their thorns*

To that one friend,

who stood by me no matter what…

# With you, I'm home

Like a beautiful butterfly fluttering its way toward a flower,
You grace me, bestowing upon me your love and care.
Like the enchanting purple in a vast spread lavender field,
You uplift me, filling me with immense joy and serenity.

Like how the moon embraces the night, you were always there,
Lending your glow to guide my way through the darkness.
Like how the gentle rain nurtures the blossoms, you enliven my spirit,
Showering me with your care and helping me blossom into my true self.

Like a carefree bird soaring in the sky, I'm myself when I'm with you,
Unburdened and unafraid, I spread my wings and

*the roses and their thorns*

revel in bliss.
Like the stars that light up the night, being with you illuminates me,
And the more I spend time with you, the more I understand myself better.

Like the first rays of the morning sun, you bring warmth and hope,
Brightening my day and filling my heart with boundless happiness.
Like a cool breeze on a hot day, being with you refreshes my soul.
Everyone else is merely words, but you are an elegantly penned poem.

*Jasmitha Alle*

You're the chapter,
whose starting page I gently fold,
A place to return to with
a sense of belonging in my heart.

*the roses and their thorns*

But your scent is not the same anymore,
your eyes are empty,
your presence feels hollow.

*Jasmitha Alle*

Why did the stars fade from our once-bright sky?
Why did everything go downhill again?

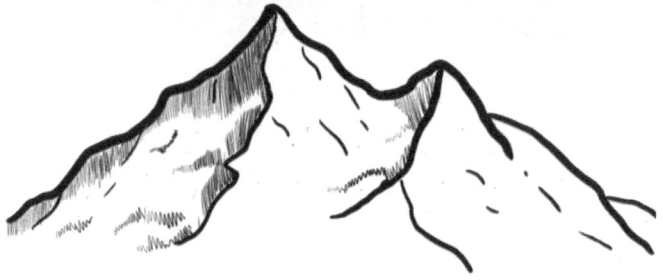

*the roses and their thorns*

Why do the whispers of our regrets resonate louder than the moments we cherished?

Would time have unfolded differently if we had chosen sorry instead of goodbye?

Could I have prevented all this if I could've talked to your heart?

*Jasmitha Alle*

## Beyond your mask

Your words, as sweet as honey,
But your heart is a hive of malevolence.
Your smile, as warm as a sunlit meadow,
But your intentions are like shadows in the night.

Your face, a beautifully painted mask,
Home to a monster lurking beneath.
Your values, a guise of generosity,
A veil, concealing the venom within.

You are as beautiful as a rose to the world,
But only I know the pain your thorns have inflicted.

*the roses and their thorns*

And as the pages of time turn,
I'm left with the chapter of our friendship torn out.

*Jasmitha Alle*

>The stars above still shine,
>but they lost their sparkle
>the day you walked away.

*the roses and their thorns*

## Yesterday

A heartfelt smile resonates in the room,
All I can hear is laughs and banters.
Happiness fills the place like radiant rays,
Chasing away all the shadows and grays.

Burdenless, unknown to worry's glare,
Embracing life with an open heart.
Living the night surrounded by pure hearts,
Their presence, a comfort, a safe haven.

Blessed with so many people I can turn to,
A circle of support, a bond we willingly share.
All of us soaring high to touch the sky,
Bound by shared dreams, together we fly.

So many feelings, like waves on the shore,
Each one distinct, yet part of the core.
New branches unfurl every time I connect,
An artwork of emotions, intricate and divine.

Always with my herd, protected,
Never neglected, never disconnected.
Wrapped in the warmth of these moments,
Another symphony plays on, its echoes potent.

*Jasmitha Alle*

Now, the silence of your absence

                              echoes louder

                                            than the laughter we shared.

*the roses and their thorns*

Our smiles have faded,
leaving behind a quiet room
filled with nothing
but
*what-ifs.*

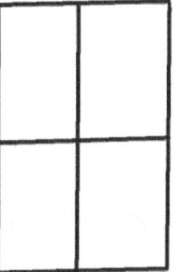

*Jasmitha Alle*

## Today

Smiling 'cause I have no one to wipe my tears,
All I can hear is the deafening silence.
Melancholy filling the place like a somber veil,
Chasing away all the brightness and colors.

Encumbered, unable to find a reason to smile,
Pushing away everything that was dear to me.
Silenced by the loud screams of loneliness,
This eerie presence, a specter, a curse.

My soul trapped within these four walls,
With no hope of letting my feelings out.
The sky now stands higher, out of reach.
Bound by doomed destinies, together we fall.

All those feelings, now extinct, hidden,
Beneath a mask of smiles, forever forbidden.
Slashed my own trunk, severing ties with the past,
Now I'm just another fallen tree, forgotten by time.

*the roses and their thorns*

Lost my way back home, isolated for another eternity,
Utterly neglected, thoroughly disconnected.
Suffocating in the venomous grasp of those moments,
Letting the past prey on me as I suffer this unceasing ache.

But I still think about the past and linger
in those moments that forever last,
in my memories,
in my heart,
in the shadows of time that refuse to depart.

*Jasmitha Alle*

Being around you hurts,
but I can't leave either.
Why did you have to make it so hard for me?

*the roses and their thorns*

Why did you show me the light when you knew you were going to leave me in the dark?

Why did you teach me to fly when you knew you were going to clip my wings one day?

Why did you plant a seed of hope when you knew you were never going to water it?

Why did you teach me how to dance when you knew you were going to silence the music?

Why did you build a bridge when you knew you were going to burn it down?

Why did you promise a sunrise when you knew you were associated with the night?

Why did you give me a taste of joy when you knew you were going to drown me in sorrow?

*Jasmitha Alle*

To the one who blossoms and fades like fleeting petals, goodbye.

*the roses and their thorns*

If all my happiness were to terminate at the end of one chapter like this,
shouldn't I just give up?

*Jasmitha Alle*

I want to.

*the roses and their thorns*

But,
aren't several chapters like these what make a book complete?

*Jasmitha Alle*

I want to try.

Though it may seem daunting,

I want to fight.

I want to give my best.

I don't want to have any regrets.

*the roses and their thorns*

And no matter who it is,
can you really be yourself with someone?

*Jasmitha Alle*

And even if you were,
will they ever truly understand you?

*the roses and their thorns*

Never trust anyone more than yourself.

*Jasmitha Alle*

*the roses and their thorns*

*Jasmitha Alle*

# Society

*the roses and their thorns*

And now,
I'm just exploring my memories,
because there is nowhere else I belong.

*Jasmitha Alle*

## Meh

Waking up to something I don't want to,
I have been breathing, but evaporating gradually.
I have become a zombie,
Just walking unconsciously.

Yesterday was a rainbow.
Never failed to leave a smile on my face,
Always something new, and everything felt right,
Everything seemed smooth.

But, today?
It's a present I didn't wish for.
Nothing's new, and nothing feels right.
All I can see is the clear, black sky.

Tomorrow?
I feel it'll also be dehydrated and drained.
Would the sky be overcast with clouds,
Ready to shoot another storm on me?

It's storming, and the weather is all blustery.
Will I also be one of those trees,
Those trees that broke apart,
Those trees that were uprooted?

*the roses and their thorns*

Everything is so peaceful in dreams,
and then I wake up to this cold reality I never wanted.

But this obstacle is yet another nightmare.
      this too shall pass,
      like clouds in the sky,
      like this moment.
      I am gonna wake up.

*the roses and their thorns*

## Used to it

Waking up to another tragedy,
Wearing a fake smile to forget it all,
Watching my life slip out of my hands,
It's like I'm used to it now.

Singing another sad song,
Sailing another voyage without a purpose,
Struggling to find a reason to live,
It's like I'm used to it now.

Celebrating another failure,
Creating a new path, just for me to get lost again,
Convincing myself it's growth,
It's like I'm used to it now.

Reading the same book again,
Running in circles, chasing the wind,
Reciting this to myself as I close my eyes,
It's like I'm used to it now.

*Jasmitha Alle*

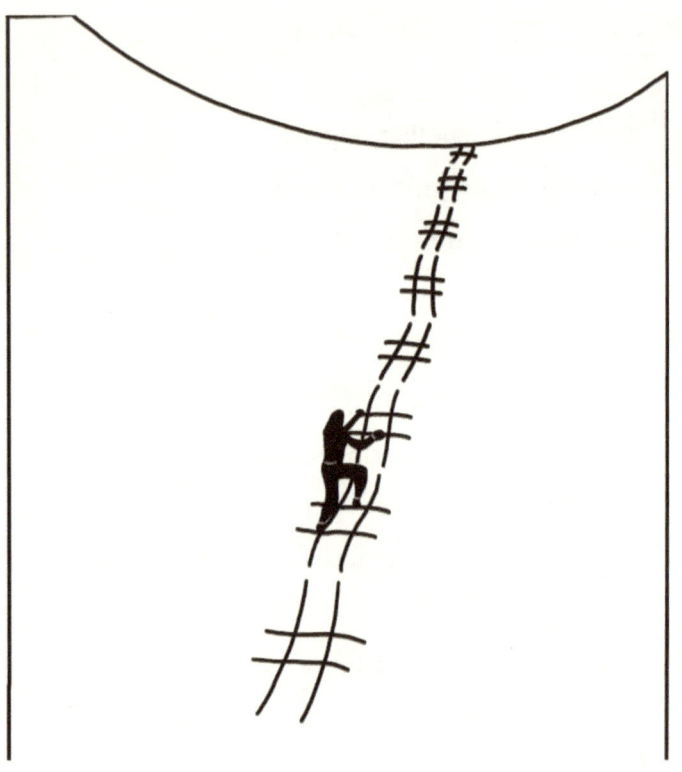

In the depth of these problems, lies the solution,
the determination to fight yet another battle,
the courage to take down the strongest monster ever.

## *the roses and their thorns*

It's all in me.

It has always been that way.

At least, that's what I'd like to think.

*Jasmitha Alle*

                                                  I ask the stars,
"Will this ever get better?"
They asked me back,
"Did you ever wake up on a day the sun never rose?"

*the roses and their thorns*

They say,
"Don't chase the clear skies.
A thunderstorm is what it takes
to become a better version of ourselves.
Ordinary is what we need to run away from."

But what do I do
when the thunderstorms seem to never end?
When the challenges keep piling up,
and I can't catch a break?

*Jasmitha Alle*

Why did laughter
stop being a daily occurrence in my life?

Why have I started associating
places and people
with stress and sorrow instead of joy?

## Silence

In the depths of isolation, a silent play unfolds,
Where shadows dance with nostalgic memories,
A safe haven where one discovers realization,
And in the stillness of time is born enlightenment.
Yet, silence is perceived as the echo of despair,
An isolated landscape, void of warmth and care.

But, silence has a voice.
It's a language of its own,
A language that embraces feelings.

When everything around you seems melancholic,
Seize the feeling of silence, let it lead you.
Within its gentle whispers lie the greatest secrets,
And the solutions to pervasive problems.
Silence is not solitude. Silence is companionship,
The only one beside you in this chaotic world.

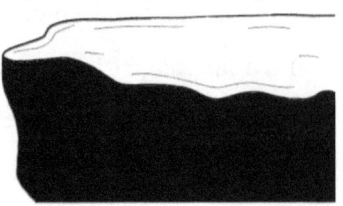

And it all disappears,
even if for a moment,
when I look up at the stars..

*the roses and their thorns*

If every tear you shed out of sorrow
is considered a curse,
then shouldn't every smile
be considered a blessing?

Honestly,

how much of our lives is

spent chasing temporary pleasures

instead of seeking lasting fulfillment?

*the roses and their thorns*

Why have we never considered how many beautiful moments we've missed while worrying about others' expectations?

*Jasmitha Alle*

And wouldn't happiness lose its meaning if we're doing something against our will?

*the roses and their thorns*

What dreams did we once hold close to our hearts that have now been buried by the demands of daily life?

*Jasmitha Alle*

Would you rather chase your dreams or chase society's expectations and wake up one day realizing you've lived a life that wasn't truly yours?

*the roses and their thorns*

Embrace dreams over norms.

Rekindle buried hopes.

Seize overlooked joys,

for genuine happiness blooms in aligned paths.

*Jasmitha Alle*

*the roses and their thorns*

*Jasmitha Alle*

# Warmth

## Spring

The deers leaping on the viridescent lawn,
The lark harmonizing with the wind,
Cherry blossoms lighting up the way,
The world, smiling and cheering, once again.

The fawns running to their mothers joyfully,
The lark pushing its limits like never before,
Spring sowing the seeds of hope and spirit,
Blooming the flowers of success and happiness.

## Summer

The ocean admiring the sun's beauty,
The sun hiding and blushing, flustered,
As it glances at its reflection in the water.
The waves whispered the story to the shore.

The ocean expanding its territory to gaze at the sun,
The sun spreading its light to the ends of the world,
The waves weaving the threads of this story together,
Summer planting the saplings of growth and gain.

## Monsoon

Thick clouds hiding the bright, blue sky,
Experiencing more darkness than light,
People locked up in their residences,
The bitter winds howl with relentless might.

Though terrifying, the thick clouds shall pass.
And there are bright places even in the darkest of times.
Though this might seem daunting and depressing,
All you need to do is find your way back home.

*Jasmitha Alle*

## Winter

A season of changes, harsh and severe,
Snowflakes blanketing the world,
Yet, in these depths of frost and cold,
A tale of resilience and courage unfolds.

And once again…

The deers leaped on the viridescent lawn,
The lark harmonized with the wind,
Cherry blossoms lit up the way,
The world smiled and cheered, once again.

The fawns ran to their mothers joyfully,
The lark pushed its limits like never before,
Spring sowed the seeds of hope and spirit,
Blooming the flowers of success and happiness.

*the roses and their thorns*

Just like the changing seasons,
life transitions in phases,

some in joy,
some in struggle and sorrow,
some in reflection.

Life is like a game.

The rules are complex,

the challenges are varied,

but the outcome is shaped by your choices.

**Lives remaining: 0**

*the roses and their thorns*

Like a persistent river,
each dawn's embrace carries us
closer to the ocean of our aspirations.
No matter the twists and turns,
the currents of time etch away the barriers in our way.

*Jasmitha Alle*

You are not defined by your weakness;
you are defined by your courage in facing it.

*the roses and their thorns*

It's okay to be afraid of heights, but it's not okay to be afraid of flying.
Soar higher.

*Jasmitha Alle*

Even the most beautiful wave sets back once it's time
but the shore doesn't mourn its departure;
it waits right there for the next wave
to bless it again.

## Life

In the midst of life,
Arises a problem, every minute,
A new difficulty rising with every step,
With every breath you take.

One stands as tall as a mountain,
Doubts spread across its crest.
Obstacles rush like a wild river's flow,
Carving scars as you strive to grow.

Other scorching and vast as a desert,
Leaving us all parched, for an eternity,
Pricked constantly by the cacti thorns,
Unable to survive another day.

Another like a maze, with twists and turns,
Lost in its corridors, our souls, our mind.
Burdens pinch in on us as we navigate,
Unable to find a way out in such a state.

But the same mountain, once daunting,
Stands as a guide, as we conquer our fears,
For the view from the summit is a sight so beautiful,
Rewarding our victory with a newfound stand.

The desert, though barren, finds its way to live,
Mirroring the resilience within.
The cacti, though thorny, find their way to survive,
Reflecting the endurance within them.

That maze, once perplexing, becomes our only hope,
Revealing the hidden treasures, awaiting us inside.
Discovering the purpose, setting our spirits free,
The only way out is to embrace the situation.

Life's difficulties, though may appear atrocious,
Are catalysts for growth, helping us to flourish through.
Whether it be mountains, deserts, or mazes,
We always find the strength to face what life brings.

## Paths unseen

Life, a voyage in uncertainty and fear,
Where destinies are woven in mystery,
Where lie the paths unseen, undiscovered,
Unveiling hidden marvels as we lead.

Beyond the horizon, a world yet unseen,
A planet of possibilities, clear and vibrant,
A new book, waiting to be opened,
A new beginning, diving into the boundless.

Sometimes life beckons us to face adversity,
And sometimes, treats us with happiness,
For in the divergence, a gift may appear,
An opportunity, precious and dear.

The light of possibility shines most bright,
When we venture into the depths of the night.
Persevere, endure, conquer, prevail,
For in the paths unseen, lie the stories untold.

*Jasmitha Alle*

How many opportunities have you let slip away because you were too afraid of failure or rejection? Do you genuinely believe that the "next time" will grace you with its presence again?

*the roses and their thorns*

All of this is about you, not them.
Don't be afraid to give it your all.

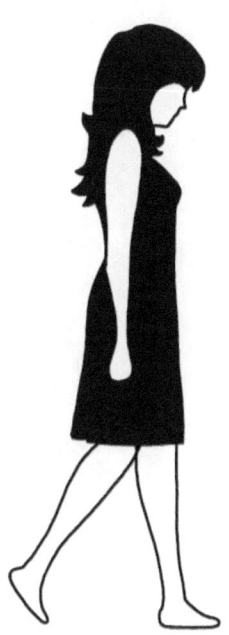

*Jasmitha Alle*

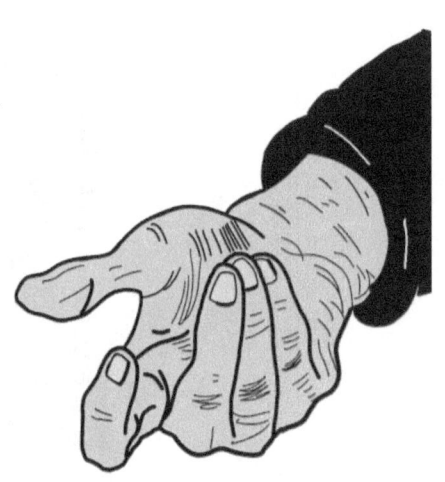

Because,
at the end of the day,
all we have is the present moment.

# Time

Time, something I wanted most to stay,
Something that never stays.
Slowly sliding like the sand in an hourglass,
Gently ticking like the hands of a clock,
Rising and setting like the sun,
Time, like a ceaseless flow of thoughts,
Never stops.

Time, something I wish I had more of,
Something that's never generous.
Time, hastily flowing like a mystic river,
You can't touch the same water once again,
You can't encounter this moment afresh,
For the flow that has passed shall never,
Pass again.

*Jasmitha Alle*

You know it might not be the same tomorrow,
> so make the most of today.

*the roses and their thorns*

And there are a lot of things you can't control.
Focus on what you can control,
Focus on making positive changes
And shaping your own path,

*Jasmitha Alle*

Because,
time loves to leave us behind
in a dark room of
*could-have-beens,*
with no way out.

*the roses and their thorns*

And this time, you can't turn the hourglass.

*Jasmitha Alle*

# Regret

Windows fogged up completely,
Resting on my rocking chair at midnight,
With a glass of wine by my side table,
Contemplating time's poignant flight.

Pondering on the roads I failed to take,
The chances I let slip out of my hands.
Mourning the words left unsaid,
Shedding tears over this painful feeling.

Staring blankly at the massive clock,
Placed on the wall right in front of me,
Wishing I could stop time, even if for a moment,
By breaking the giant hands of this clock.

This feeling etched deep in my chest,
The moments squandered, lost in time,
Reverberate every single day, consistently,
In this regretful heart of mine.

I long to turn back the hands of fate,
To rewrite this story, to repaint this canvas,
To retake this step, to alter my state,
To pave a path where this feeling finds its end.

*the roses and their thorns*

Regret is a cruel teacher, a bitter encounter.
Its lessons taught in sorrow and despair,
Yet a glimmer of hope, in its grasp,
A chance to seek a better place.

*Jasmitha Alle*

Regret, the unwelcomed companion in strife,
Presents itself to teach us the value of life,
For in each stumble, there lies a chance,
And in each wound, there lies a cure.

*the roses and their thorns*

And if you knew today was your last day,
what would be your biggest regret
and why haven't you addressed it yet?

## Rewind

Those adorable giggles, snuggles with stuffed animals,
Wobbly first steps, blowing bubbles in the park,
Rewinding to those happy moments from childhood.
Cuddling with parents at bedtime, running through sprinklers,
No feeling of embarrassment, but just fun and pleasure.
Learning to draw our favorite superhero for the first time ever,
Excited for our little candy treat, proud of our accomplishment.
How I wish I could turn back time.

*the roses and their thorns*

But as we grow and learn,
we have new challenges at hand.
With each passing day, we grow more wise,
and our journey becomes a wonderful surprise,
with endless possibilities in sight.

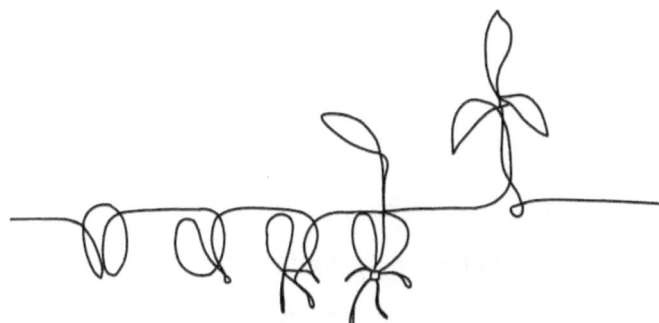

*Jasmitha Alle*

Falling can be beautiful when you give it all you've got.
The greatest proof is the falling stars,
and the leaves shed by trees during autumn.

*the roses and their thorns*

And one day, the final chapter was written.

## The end

In the twilight of our days, as our shadows part with us,
We embrace the ending with a longing glance.
The end of a beautiful book, the end of a memorable dream,
These moments are to be cherished for years to come.
Through lines etched upon our weathered face,
A drapery woven with wisdom and grace.
The battles fought, the wars won, the victories achieved,
A life well-lived, a journey now comes to an end.
The sun finally sets on this mortal plane,
But our souls soar, forever unwavering, forever unbending,
For in our hearts, burns a bright flame, endlessly ablaze,
Illuminating our sacred paths to eternal light.
As we travel from our cradle to our grave,
We accomplish a lot, we lose a lot, we learn a lot,
But at the end, we're all just stars in the sky,
Just some brighter than the others.

*the roses and their thorns*

It ~~was~~ is the end.

*Jasmitha Alle*

Chase your stars, mate. Life is short.

*the roses and their thorns*

Finally,

*Jasmitha Alle*

I know you know it all, but have you realized it yet?

*the roses and their thorns*

:)

## Conclusion

As we reach the end of this collection, we find ourselves at the culmination of a poetic journey that has delved deep into the realms of human emotion. Each poem has been a glimpse into the spectrum of feelings that paint our lives — from the soft strokes of happiness to the bold strokes of grief.

Just as individual notes come together to compose a symphony, each piece in this anthology has contributed to the intricate mosaic of shared human experiences. From the heights of exuberance to the quiet corners of self-discovery, these poems endeavor to mirror the rhythm of our innermost sentiments.

In this concluding passage, I extend an invitation for you to carry these lines forward, allowing them to linger like echoes in your thoughts. For just as the ink flows beyond these pages, poetry meanders through the corridors of life, a companion for the myriad encounters that await. May these words continue to reverberate, ignite inspiration, and offer solace as you navigate the unwritten chapters of your journey.

With heartfelt gratitude for your companionship through these verses, I bid you adieu, dear reader, until destiny reunites us again

## Acknowledgement

I want to express my heartfelt thanks to my mom and dad, whose unwavering support and love have been my guiding light.

Mom and Dad, your belief in me has been my driving force. Your sacrifices and love have shaped me into who I am today. Your constant presence has taught me the value of determination and chasing after my dreams. With every step I take, I remember your teachings and values. Your faith has given me strength even in tough times. You've shown me that challenges can be overcome and that pursuing what you're passionate about is a journey worth taking.

This book is a tribute to your love and sacrifices. I'm grateful for all you've done, the wisdom you've shared, and the love you've given me.

As you read these words, I hope you can feel the depth of my gratitude. Thank you for being there for me and for giving me the courage to reach for the stars.
With all my love,
Jasmitha Alle.

To my parents who have always supported me and believed in me…

*the roses and their thorns*

## Ma

She endured that first cry of mine,
After carrying me all nine.
Through sleepless nights,
A love so pure.

Healing, her gaze,
A safe haven, her embrace.
Fighting life's odds, her gentle touch,
Shaping this life of mine.

Her words of wisdom, like diamonds they shine,
Guiding me through life's complex journey.
In her eyes, a bright sparkle,
Reflecting her unconditional love.

For all the sacrifices, for all the time,
I'm always grateful in this heart of mine.
Here I stand, forever indebted to,
A mother's love, eternally divine.

*Jasmitha Alle*

## Daddy

His love transcends all distance and time,
His heart, so warm, a shelter,
His ideals, a guiding light, a strength,
His love, so deep, so true.

He's a candle that burns itself,
To light up the life of his family,
A pillar that stays strong,
Despite the vicissitudes.

He's a mountain that stands high,
Despite life's strong storm,
A caterpillar that transforms itself
Into a beautiful butterfly.

Day or night, now or a decade later,
His love and care is always unwavering.
Through laughter and tears, he's always there,
Like the sun and the moon, come what may.

## ABOUT THE AUTHOR

Jasmitha Alle was born in 2006 in India. With a deep-rooted appreciation for authenticity, confidence, and resilience, Jasmitha explores a range of emotions that resonate with readers far and wide. Beyond poetry, dance, and art stand as her companions, offering her both solace and creativity. *The roses and their thorns* is Jasmitha's first book.

*Jasmitha Alle*

# CONNECT WITH THE POET

Email: jasmithaalle@gmail.com

*the roses and their thorns*

Copyright © 2023 Jasmitha Alle

All rights reserved. No part of this book may be reproduced or used in any manner without the prior written permission of the copyright owner, except for the use of brief quotations in a book review.

www.ingramcontent.com/pod-product-compliance
Lightning Source LLC
LaVergne TN
LVHW092049060526
838201LV00047B/1301